cat
gatto

rabbit

coniglio

dog

cane

chick

pulcino

duck
anatra

sheep

pecora

goat

capra

pig

maiale

donkey

asino

horse

cavallo

cow

mucca

mouse

topo

bat

pipistrello

bee

ape

spider

ragno

fox

volpe

deer

cervo

squirrel

scoiattolo

hedgehog

riccio

owl

gufo

frog

rana

snake
serpente

racoon

procione

parrot

pappagallo

toucan

tucano

alligator

alligatore

sea turtle

tartaruga marina

flamingo

fenicottero

penguin

pinguino

crab

granchio

jellyfish

medusa

seal

foca

shark

squalo

whale

balena

orca

orca

starfish
stella marina

rhinoceros

rinoceronte

panda

panda

monkey

scimmia

lion

leone

tiger

tigre

elephant

elefante

www.ingramcontent.com/pod-product-compliance
Lightning Source LLC
LaVergne TN
LVHW071626180726
843512LV00002B/258